Forty Days of Prayer: Preparing Ourselves for God's Calling

Mark Tidsworth

CONTENTS

FORTY DAYS OF PRAYER

This prayer guide is designed to prepare Christian disciples for discerning God's calling for their lives and for their congregation. Each day's guide includes a scripture reading, devotional thought related to spiritual discernment and a prayer thought. These daily guides are grouped by themes:

Starting Well – Praying In Faith
Christian Deformation–Laying Aside Distractions
Christian Formation – Growing More Christ-Centered
Discerning God's Calling – Opening Oneself to God's Direction

You are invited to pray every day, for the next 40 days, for yourself as a Christian disciple and for your church, as the gathered community of disciples. You are also invited to join a prayer triad, praying together for yourselves and for your congregation. A guide for your prayer triad is found toward the end of this booklet.

When disciples and churches embrace this process, they prepare themselves for discerning God's call…discerning God's vision. May you encounter the Living God through your praying these next 40 days!

Rev. Mark Tidsworth, President
Pinnacle Leadership Associates

MARK TIDSWORTH

1 STARTING WELL: PRAYING IN FAITH

God invites us to pray! According to the Scriptures, God encourages frequent praying. We are encouraged to come to God in prayer, just as we are...but we rarely leave sincere prayer staying the same. Embrace this opportunity. Engage your Lord these 40 days with faith. Trust that God will act, with this Season of Prayer as a channel of God's love.

Day 1- Disciples of Jesus Christ

Luke 5:27-28

"Follow me."

How simple Jesus' call to discipleship really is…. simple, short, direct, invitational. Some of the first invitees were delighted that such an important Rabbi would invite them to follow. Others, when they learned more about Jesus' teachings, said, "no thanks." Imagine Jesus Christ looking directly at you, inviting you to make him Lord of your entire life, and saying, "Come on, follow me."

As you begin this spiritual journey, where you start is important. What do you do with Jesus' invitation? How important is it for you? What would it mean for your life if you answered Jesus' call at a deeper level and a more significant way than ever before? What does fully devoted discipleship look like for you?

Prayer Thought: What does it mean for me to live as a disciple of Jesus Christ?

Day 2 – Gathering Around the Messiah

Matthew 16:13-20

That's it. That's the confession we gather around: "You are the Messiah, the Son of the living God." This is the confession, the awareness, the foundation that God builds the Church upon. God commissioned a living, breathing organism called the Church to live out this confession day by day. Jesus is very confident in the Church's perseverance and power...nothing can stand against it; nothing can deter its purpose from being accomplished.

You are the Church, which Jesus established. You are part of God's body in the world. Rejoice!

Prayer Thought: Lord, what makes a church a church? First, it is a group of people gathered around Christ, staking their lives on the confession of Jesus as Lord. But then what?

Day 3 – Praying In Faith

Matthew 7:7-11

Ask – Search – Knock. Jesus paints a picture of a loving parent who wants to give good gifts to his/her children. We parents can relate to that. We naturally want to provide well for our children, giving them every advantage in life we can. We hope this will equip them with a good beginning to a long and happy life.

God wants the same for us. How willing are you to pray with faith, with anticipation, with trust that God will answer? Do you believe in prayer as a spiritual discipline, which influences you and others? Are you willing to pray in a way that makes you vulnerable to the prayer's answer?

Prayer Thought: Describe to God your perspective on prayer. Consider inviting God to grow your faith as you pray.

Day 4 – Limited By Unbelief

Mark 6:1-6

Jesus was limited by their unbelief. Surely God can do great deeds without the belief of humankind as an ingredient in the mix! Surely so. But it appears as if <u>God has chosen</u> to include the faith of disciples as an ingredient in the mix. Why? We don't exactly know.

For some reason, God wanted to include disciples in God's mission of redemption and transformation. Prayer is a primary tool of this work.

Perhaps we can hold God back when we think small or skeptically about what can happen. Our unbelief, along with our belief, is part of the mix. Since that is so, our trust and faith actually influence the success of God's mission. How do you feel about that?

Prayer Thought: Consider what you believe God cannot do in you and in your church. Consider surrendering this belief to God.

Day 5- Starting Where You Are

John 3:1-10, John 7:45-52, John 19:38-39

Nicodemus. At first he was curious...he saw something in Jesus worth pursuing. Then he cautiously defended Jesus against some of his Pharisee colleagues. The last picture we see of Nicodemus in the Bible is of an openly supportive disciple, preparing Jesus' body for burial. Nicodemus' conversion to Christ appears to have evolved over time, becoming a disciple step by step. He began with curiosity, became a seeker, and then a full-blown disciple.

Like Nicodemus, we are a work in progress. As we are conformed to the image of Christ, our attitudes and motives shift. You may wonder how pure your motives are as you pray for yourself and your church. You may question if you just want what you want...and not what God wants. Don't let this fear (or awareness) hold you back. Don't wait until your motives are completely pure. Start praying, in humility and faith, and ask God to help your motives and agendas to grow more Christ-like. Start where you are and trust God to move you forward. It is easier to guide a moving ship, than one roped to the dock.

Prayer Thought: Consider asking God to purify your motives for you and for your church, even while you are praying the best you can at this moment.

Day 6 - Faith: Small Quantities Will Do

Luke 17:1-6

While Jesus is informing the disciples that forgiving those who wrong us is a requirement of Christian discipleship, the disciples are growing overwhelmed. "How is this humanly possible?" is the question behind their request for more faith. Jesus essentially tells them that only a very small quantity of faith is needed for accomplishing great things in God's kingdom.

If all we need are small quantities, then where do we get our supply? Even this God will supply. God will give you what you need to do what God wants done. So, if you want more faith, ask – seek – knock – and trust that God will give you the amount of faith needed.

Prayer Thought: Consider asking God to increase your faith. The disciples before you felt the need to ask Jesus for more faith...and they were looking the Messiah in the eye. Surely it is a good request for those who have come along 2000 years later.

Day 7 - Praying As Influence

James 5:13-18

Yes, the prayer of the righteous is powerful and effective. But who among us is righteous? (Those who think they are certainly aren't) Righteousness comes from God. Righteous is how God sees us when we are washed clean by the sacrificial love of the Lord Jesus Christ. So, when we are in Christ, we are righteous. So, how does that influence your praying? Are you aware that your praying influences God's movement in your life and in the life of your church?

Prayer Thought: Consider believing your praying will make more difference than you have ever believed before. Pray today with that awareness.

Day 8 - Shalom Practicing

John 14: 25-27

"..my peace I give to you." Whenever we pray with sincerity and openness, change happens. We follow a God who is on the move; on mission in the world. This awareness can raise anxiety. What will happen when we pray? What will be asked of us as individuals and as a congregation? Will my life become miserable? I hope you are asking these questions. If not, perhaps you don't grasp the ramifications of praying. Praying will bring change.

Is there guidance for us around these questions? Certainly. As Jesus prepared his disciples for his departure, he informed them they would be filled with his peace. They had observed him, sharing life together, as they travelled across the Middle-East landscape. Obviously, Jesus had a source of peace that exceeded human calmness. This is the peace Jesus promised them.

Prayer Thought: Bring your anxiety about praying for God's will to God. Remember Jesus' promise to those first disciples. Ask God for whatever level of peace you need in order to engage prayer with confidence and joy.

Day 9 – Praying With Confidence

Hebrews 4:14-16

"Been there, done that," is a saying Jesus can use to describe the human experience. There is no challenge, difficulty or temptation with which Jesus our Brother cannot sympathize. However hard you experience life, or temptation, or challenge to be...Jesus has been there. We follow a Savior who is experienced in the human dilemma.

Jesus has cleared the way through his triumph over sin. So, we can approach God with confidence, boldness and anticipation. God invites us to do so! Pray for yourself, for your loved ones, for the world with gusto. Jesus says, "Bring it on."

Prayer Thought: Don't hold back. Ask God for what you and your church need in order to fulfill your callings.

2 CHRISTIAN DEFORMATION: LAYING ASIDE DISTRACTIONS

Christian mystics call the process of laying down our wills and taking up God's will "Deformation." This is an accurate description of the experience. We have built up layer upon layer of control and self-direction. The process of becoming a disciple is submitting ourselves to God's refinement. God strips away these layers of denial, sin and selfishness. The process feels like we are being de-formed. The result...then we are far more open to being re-formed as disciples of Jesus Christ.

Day 10 - The Prayer of Surrender

Luke 22:39-46

"Father, is there any other way?" Jesus knew that his mission involved laying down his life. His humanity did not want to give up control over his destiny. Who in his/her right mind would want to endure suffering? Jesus knew what was coming, and he did not want to go through it. Father, is there any other way?

Regardless of the anticipated suffering, Jesus was willing to lay down his will for the Father's will. God's way is better. How much do we believe (and practice) that? God's way is better for you as an individual, and for your church community.

Prayer Thought: Ask God what in your life needs the Prayer of Surrender, and then consider praying it in faith. Consider sharing this prayer with another disciple who you trust and would be supportive of your prayer.

Day 11 - Letting Go And Taking Hold

Hebrews 11:1-3

The trapeze artist makes a decision to let go before she experiences the reassurance of the "catch." At just the right time, she commits to the flight. There is no turning back then. Free-flying follows...until the catch is made.

Before we can take hold of God's hopes and dreams for us, we must let go of our comforts, securities and aspirations. We have to let go, flying through the air, trusting that God is there to make the catch. This is what faith is about.

Prayer Thought: Ask God to identify what you are clutching that prevents you letting go. Then ask God for the courage to let go and fly.

Day 12 - Crucified With Christ

Galatians 2: 19-20

"I have been crucified with Christ." What does this mean? Are our personalities and personhood wiped away? No. These are gifts from God. Instead being crucified with Christ is more about laying down our wills. By accepting the way of the cross, Jesus accepted and lived the Father's will rather than his own. This is what being crucified with Christ means for us too. We are called to live out God's values, ways, and mission in this world.

Years ago, the most Christ-like person I know, shared his secret with me. "Before I get out of bed in the morning," he said. "I lay down my life again, and ask God to fill me with the Holy Spirit. I commit each day, one day at a time, to God. Essentially, I am crucified with Christ again each day. If I don't do that (and even do it repeatedly during each day), then I take charge of everything again."

Prayer Thought: How about an experiment? Consider praying like my friend does...before your feet hit the floor in the morning. You could try this for one day, or one week, or one month and then reflect on how God moves through this experience.

Day 13- Forgetting Your Credentials

Philippians 3:3-9

Becoming and being competent is a great experience. Most of us train, learn, and develop our skills over time, becoming competent in many activities: vocational skills, sports, relational expertise, homemaking, etc. There is great joy in being competent.

When it comes to formation as faithful disciples, competence is a liability. When we believe ourselves worthy of God's approval, because of our merits, then we shut God out. The Apostle Paul was religiously competent, a religious expert no less. But he gave all that up for the pure grace of God. In fact, he was willing to give up everything, for the joy of knowing Christ. In comparison with life in Christ, all his accomplishments seem like garbage. When we are in Christ, life is sweet.

Prayer Thought: Are you competent in God? No? Great. God is competent in you; in redeeming you. Consider asking God to purify your reliance on God's grace as the source of your life energy.

Day 14 - Mental Models of Church

Acts 2:43-47

What's a good church? What's an effective church? How do we know we are on track? Every Christian person (and most others too) have a picture of a "good" church in their minds. This picture is developed from many experiences, sermons, mentors and cultural influences. In order to discern God's vision for your congregation, you must let go of this picture...whatever it is...as much as you can. It's not that this mental model is wrong or bad – It's simply that it is <u>your</u> mental model for the church. Even this needs to be laid at the feet of Jesus.

Prayer Thought: "Lord, what is it in my mental model that gets in your way?"

Day 15 - The Happiness Trap

Luke 9:21-27

Church consultant Gil Rendle writes about "The Happiness Trap." When our goal in church life is to keep as many people as happy or pleased as much of the time as possible...then we are in the happiness trap. Is this what Jesus gave his life for? For us to be pleased with how our church is running? Is it about our comfort and contentment? When we look at the Jesus we see in the Gospels, we don't see a Savior overly concerned with the personal preferences or comfort of his disciples.

Prayer Thought: Reflect with God on how you evaluate church. If not the happiness of the members, then what is it about?

Day 16- It's Not About You

Philippians 2:3-5

Perhaps Rick Warren read this Philippians passage before he made this saying popular, "It's not about you." Everything in our culture tells us the opposite. Get all you can and enjoy it. Whoever has the most toys at the game's end is the winner. These are the beliefs of popular culture. Most of us bring that attitude to church with us. We want church like we want it...now. If not, we will be Christian consumers, and go elsewhere. Thankfully, church is not about us!

Prayer Thought: Thank God that church is one place or community in the world that is not focused on pleasing you – but has a much higher purpose.

Day 17 - Building On The Sand

Matthew 7:24-27

"If you find the perfect church, don't join it...you will ruin it for everyone else." We are imperfect people, so when we get together in groups, we form imperfect groups. Church is no exception. Hopefully we manage our imperfections in the life of the church with more grace than other organizations, but we will never be perfect in church.

Given this awareness, what is it about our church that really does not reflect Christ's spirit or mission? What are the attitudes or expectations that are not based in Christ? What do we do that may be nice, or enjoyable, or interesting, but really does not advance God's kingdom? These things are built on the sand. We may need to let them go, preventing them from draining our resources as God's people.

Prayer Thought: What in our church life may be built on sand?

Day 18 - Listening More Than Talking

I Kings 19:11-13

How does God speak to you? God speaks in many ways. How are we supposed to hear, understand, or discern God's voice when we do all the talking? Sometimes God speaks in a still, small voice. The breezes of the Spirit are sometimes soft and subtle, just brushing the face. God may be whispering, or blowing, or otherwise communicating to you today.

Prayer Thought: Consider quieting your soul, and then spending your prayer time today in silent listening. Whenever a thought intrudes, take note of it, and then let it pass on through. Make space for God's voice.

3 CHRISTIAN FORMATION:
GROWING MORE CHRIST-CENTERED

As the old, sinful self is left behind, God helps us build a more Christ-centered self. We become new creations. We move toward the abundant life Jesus came to bring. Our thought processes are transformed and our desires become more Christ-focused. We are transformed more and more into the image of Christ. As you pray, allow yourself to become more the person you are called to be.

Day 19 – Being Sure Whose You Are

I Corinthians 1:22-23

God has laid claim to you. God has adopted you into his family. God has put his seal on you (branded you so to speak), and has given you his Spirit. It is unmistakable who's you are. Rest in this awareness. Realize this reality. Know that nothing can take you away from God once God has made you his own.

Prayer Thought: Remember the loneliest time in your life...know now that you will never be alone. God is always with you and has given you the church as his earthly presence. Thank God.

Day 20 – God Loves You...Period.

John 3:16

Phillip Yancey reminds us that we cannot do anything to influence God to love us more. And, we cannot do anything to make God love us less. God's love is not based on how good or bad we are. God's love is based on the character of God. So, receive it. Quit trying to earn it or rebelling to prove you don't need it. Stop, and receive God's love deep down in your bones.

Prayer Thought: God, to receive your love at a deeper level, I have to let go. Help me to trust you that much.

Day 21 – God Has a Calling For You To Fulfill

Ephesians 2:10

"Luke, it is your destiny." Before Luke Skywalker and Star Wars came along, we Christian disciples have known about destiny…calling, we call it. Yes, God loves and accepts us, just as we are…and then God has something for us to do. You have a calling as an individual. Your congregation has a calling to be the church in its particular place and time. Part of "working out your salvation" is to discover this individual calling and congregational calling.

Prayer Thought: Ask God to give you the eyes to see and the ears to hear his calling for you and for your congregation.

Day 22 - The Organizing Principle

Philippians 3:12-14

Successful corporations, educational institutions, and other organizations are gathered around at least one Organizing Principle. This principle gives direction to activities, decisions and goals. When times get tough or when stress is high, this principle gives guidance and provides stability.

When being formed as disciples who live in the Way of Jesus Christ, the call of God in Christ Jesus becomes our Organizing Principle. We orient our lives around Jesus Christ. Our family, career, finances, and relationships reflect this Organizing Principle. Is this too much to ask of Christian disciples?

Prayer Thought: Is Jesus Christ my Organizing Principle? How much is Jesus Christ the center of my life and my church? Ask God to help you orient your entire life more around Christ.

Day 23 – Transformed People

Romans 12:1-2, Romans 8:28-30

The Christian Deformation process is working to not become conformed to this world's values, actions and perspective. The Christian Formation process is becoming conformed to the image of Christ. What does becoming more Christ-like mean for you? As you become more Christ-like even today, how (specifically) will that show up in your life?

Prayer Thought: Ask God to transform you. Ask God to show you what new values, actions and perspectives to embrace.

Day 24 – The Great Commandment

John 13:31-35

Jesus did not give new laws, rules or policies. He was not very specific with instructions about how to live out our faith. Instead, Jesus focused on what is essential....loving each other. The first and foremost way others will know that we are disciples is our love for one another. Anything that prevents, distracts or otherwise diminishes this purpose needs to go. Loving other Christian disciples is a primary focus when we want to live as Christian people and congregations.

Prayer Thought: Confess any bitterness or resentment you hold toward fellow disciples. Ask God to strengthen your resolve to love other disciples. Ask God to help your church become more loving.

Day 25 – The Great Commission

Matthew 28:16-20

Remarkable. It is remarkable that God trusts us enough to include us in God's mission in the world. Making Disciples. First we are called to love other disciples and then to participate in making additional disciples. This means bringing new people into the Faith and then strengthening and supporting them in their Christian Formation process. This is our commission. This is what Christ has called us to do. This is a mark of a Christ-centered disciple and church.

Prayer Thought: Consider how much you personally are participating in this commission from Christ. Consider how focused your church is on making and forming disciples.

Day 26 – Criteria For Success

Matthew 25:31-46

Buildings, Bodies and Budgets. Sometimes disciples mistake these tangible and visible items as what makes for a successful church. The more we have of each, the more successful we are. Instead, these are simply means to the real foci – faithfulness and transformation. Becoming more like Jesus is the goal. Loving each other and making disciples are our callings. How do you measure success in your church?

Prayer Thought: Ask God to help you lay aside human criteria for church success and to integrate God's criteria more fully.

Day 27 – Trust God For What You Need

Philippians 4:10-19

Do we have what it takes to love others and make disciples? Can our church become more of what God is calling it to become? Many disciples through the centuries have asked this question…and have found that God is faithful. God will provide everything you need to do what God asks you to do. God will equip your congregation to live out its calling from God. All your needs for the journey will be supplied as they are needed. Trust God with your and your congregation's needs.

Prayer Thought: How much do I believe God will equip our congregation with what we need to accomplish God's purpose for us? Boldly ask God to dramatically increase your faith in this area.

4 DISCERNING GOD'S CALLING: OPENING ONESELF TO GOD'S CALLING

You have been preparing yourself to see, hear and otherwise discern God's calling for you and for your congregation. God does not withhold his guidance. Instead, God waits for the fullness of time, which includes us being ready to receive God's calling. Now is the time. Look to the future. Open yourself to God's voice, God's nudging, God's direction. May you receive God's direction with joy and thanksgiving.

Day 28 – The Desires Of Your Heart

Psalm 37:3-5

This scripture has always puzzled me. God will give you the desires of your heart? Won't that turn God into Santa Claus? Not when we first "Take delight in the Lord." When we center our lives in Christ, laying aside our sinful ways and selfish desires, then we discover that our hearts begin to beat like God's. Our focus grows more Christ-like. In fact, our desires change to become more Christ-like. So, in discerning God's calling for you and for your church, listen to your desires as you pray. What wisdom and guidance is there?

Prayer Thought: O Lord, as I submit myself to you as Lord of all, help me discern the desires of my heart that are reflective of your guidance.

Day 29 – Follow The Energy

Acts 2: 1-4

The Holy Spirit first came to disciples as a rushing wind, filled with energy. The Holy Spirit still enlivens us for service and ministry. Where is the energy rising up in you when it comes to following Christ? Where is the energy rising up in your church these days? These are clues to God's guidance and direction.

Prayer Thought: Look for the energy in you and your church rising up. Ask God if these are clues to God's calling.

Day 30 - Gathered Community of Disciples

Acts 2:43-47

When Jesus' disciples band together in groups, what do they do? How do they relate to each other? What distinguishes who they are as a group? What do they do with their combined resources? What's their purpose for being? What's their mission?

In this scripture, it is apparent that our faith began as a movement, with minimal institutionalization. Through the course of history, the movement took on structure, professional leadership, and property. Sometimes it's difficult not to confuse these structures with the actual purpose for the church. What is essential to being a church? What can we learn from the early Christian movement?

Prayer Thought: Ask God what is essential for your church to be, do, and become. If you don't do anything else, what 3 activities must you do to fulfill your calling as a church?

Day 31 – Consistent With Holy Scripture

II Timothy 3:16-17

It is possible for a church to follow its desires and do something inconsistent with God's mission in the world. When our desires are not shaped by Christ, they can lead us onto tangents. One purpose of the Scriptures is to provide a check and balance for us. Is the vision we are seeing consistent with what we see in the Bible? Is this vision lining up with the Great Commandment and the Great Commission? Is this vision congruent with the ministry and teachings of Jesus in the Gospels?

Prayer Thought: Ask God for insight into the meaning of scripture as compared with the emerging vision for you and your congregation.

Day 32 – Your God Is Too Small

Psalm 148

J.B. Phillips wrote a book by that title (Your God Is Too Small) in 1961. He describes how we have limited God – making God "man-sized." Our temptation is to make God in our image, rather than vice-versa. Consider the vision that's developing for you and for your church. How expansive is it? Is it something you and your church can do without God's intervention or power? If it can be done by human strength alone….then it is too small.

Prayer Thought: Ask God if you are unconsciously limiting the Vision by your small thinking about God's capacity and intervention.

Day 33 – On Earth As It Is In Heaven

Matthew 6:9-15

Did he mean it? Did Jesus actually want us to pray, with faith and trust in the possibility, that God's kingdom could come on earth as it is in heaven? Evidently, God wants his kingdom of peace, justice and love to be enacted right here, right now. What would it mean for God's kingdom to come more fully through you? Through your church?

Prayer Thought: Ask God to help you focus on kingdom work. Ask God what your church can do to help the kingdom come more fully.

Day 34 – God's Hopes And Dreams

Matthew 6:9-15

God's Will....in essence...God's desires, hopes, dreams, wishes for this world. What does it look like when a disciple lives life according to God's desires for him/her? What does it look like for your church? Your church cannot be everything to everyone, nor can it meet every need in your community. It is also true that your church has an identity, and has a God-given purpose in your community. Identify your congregation's God-given identity and its purpose....and you are very close to discerning God's vision for your congregation.

Prayer Thought: What, if taken away, would make this church no longer who it is? What is our congregation's unique opportunity in our community?

Day 35 – Living In The Zone

Matthew 11:28-30

How can God's calling for us be easy? Or God's burden be light? When I was a runner, we would plan our training to help us "peak" at just the right time in the season. We all experientially knew what it was to "peak." This is the zone...it's the time when we feel like we could run forever, when running seems almost effortless, when we can accelerate into a higher gear, when we are almost floating or flying. This is the time when personal records are set...we are in the zone.

When our lives and our churches are aligned with God's intentions and purposes, we find the zone. We are living at our "peak" so to speak. Following Christ seems nearly effortless and everything flows. This is when we get a "sneak peek" into what heaven must be like.

Prayer Thought: We can't make peak experience happen. On the other hand we can participate with God to ready ourselves. Ask God to lead you and your church into the future with courage and faith.

Day 36 – Courage To Go There

Joshua 1:1-9

"You don't want to go there." – A common warning that you are about to get into unpleasant territory. When it comes to discerning God's vision, the motto is, "You do want to go there!" Though it may seem expansive, scary and daunting at first, following God into the future is exhilarating and fulfilling. Yes, you will serve at a higher level and you will face challenges. The challenges we face when we are in the center of God's will are very acceptable. God will provide the courage you need. Go there!

Prayer Thought: Consider what you need to go there. Ask God for the courage.

Day 37 – Come to Macedonia

Acts 16:6-10

There are people in this world who actually need you and your church to discern the Vision for moving ahead. They need this because they are spiritually seeking, personally hurting or in need in some other way that you and your congregation can address. Discerning the Vision is not simply so you will know what to do. Discerning the Vision is so that God's kingdom will be implemented and real people with real needs will be saved and helped.

Prayer Thought: Ask God to help you and your congregation remain focused on God's mission rather than your comfort.

Day 38 – A Time To Work

Colossians 3:23-24

"Whatever your task, put yourselves into it.." There is a time for everything. You are nearing the time for your congregation when the Vision will be identified and celebrated. Then comes the most vital part – implementing. There is real work to be done.

Are you motivated by a challenge? If the challenge it too high, it can be demotivating, leading to apathy or resignation. If the challenge is too low, we grow lethargic. When the challenge is on target, God's people rise up and fulfill their calling to be the people of God in this place at this time.

Prayer Thought: Ask God for willingness to roll up your sleeves and get busy with God's calling for your congregation!

Day 39– Are We Done Already?

I Thessalonians 5:1-11

When I was a child, I heard older people talking about how quickly life goes. I thought they had lapsed into insanity or dementia. Did they realize how long it took for Christmas to roll around each year; or one's birthday? It's funny how a few years can change one's perspective.

The way time goes, soon we will all be reflecting back on our lives. What did we do? What contribution did we make? What was our contribution to God's kingdom and God's movement in the world?

How were we church to one another and to our part of the world?

Prayer Thought: This is your time, your moment, your opportunity to go for it. Ask God for a compelling vision and for the resources to live it out day by day.

Day 40 – Naming, Claiming, Being, Doing

Acts 2:14-21

Later in the Visioning process, the time will come to articulate the congregation's Vision, to Claim it as your own and then to live into it. That will be the time to set the hesitancy aside and serve with spiritual vigor. Prepare yourself now to embrace God's calling for you and your congregation.

Prayer Thought: Consider committing yourself to God's calling for you and your church right now...even before you know exactly what it looks like.

5 PRAYER TRIADS

Starting Well

Have you been in a prayer group or had prayer partners before? Share with your triad about that experience.

Describe your perspective and feelings about engaging in this 40 Days of Prayer experience at this point.

Look over Days 1 – 9 in this booklet. What truth or insight about prayer is most encouraging to you? Share this with your triad.

Read Luke 6:12 and I Thessalonians 5:17. Discuss the meaning of these two verses.

Share any personal concerns you would like your triad to pray about. Commit yourselves to praying for your church daily.

Take turns praying for yourselves and for your church, especially that this 40 Days of Prayer will spiritually prepare everyone for spiritual discernment.

Schedule your next prayer triad time.

Christian Deformation

Consider a time when you had to let go of something you liked and valued in order to achieve a greater good or purpose. Share this with your triad.

Discuss what the 40 Days of Prayer has been like for you so far.

Look over days 10-18 in this guide. What truths or insights are standing out for you? Share these with your triad.

Read Galatians 5:22-26. Discuss the meaning of verses 24 and 25…what does it mean to die to self and live to Christ?

As you become more Christ-centered, what attitude, behavior, or anything else might you need to let go? Share with your triad.

Pray for each other specifically. Then pray that your church will let go of what it needs to let go of, in order to be open to God's guidance into a new future.

Schedule your next prayer triad.

Christian Formation

Describe the best gift you have ever received (apart from Christ). What did that add to your life?

Discuss what the 40 Days of Prayer has been like for you so far.

Look over Days 19-27 in this guide. What insights or truths are standing out for you?

Read Romans 12:1-2. What does it mean to become transformed as Christian disciples?

What excites you about knowing you are becoming a different person? What excites you about knowing your church is entering a time of transformation?

Share any other prayer concerns you have and pray for yourselves and for your church.

Schedule your next prayer triad.

Discerning God's Calling

How did you find your vocational calling? Share with your triad.

Discuss what the 40 Days of Prayer has been like for you so far.

Look over days 28-40. What insights or truths are standing out for you as you pray and read scripture?

What clues are you gaining about God's calling for you and/or for your church? What clues are your fellow disciples getting?

Share any concerns and pray for yourselves and your church.

Thank each other for sharing this 40 Days of Prayer together. Feel free to continue meeting for prayer as you see fit!

Made in the USA
Columbia, SC
28 June 2018